PASTA

W9-CFZ-713

ROASTED TOMATO SAUCE WITH FETTUCCINE AND HERBS

4 lbs (1.8 kg) fresh FLORIDA tomatoes
¼ cup (60 ml) olive oil
¼ tsp (1 ml) black pepper, ground
½ cup (120 ml) onions, chopped
1 tbs (15 ml) garlic, minced
1 tsp (5 ml) oregano leaves, crushed
2 tbs (30 ml) white wine, or chicken broth
1 tbs (15 ml) fresh parsley, chopped
⅛ tsp (.5 ml) red pepper, crushed
1 tsp (5 ml) salt
8 oz (240 g) fettuccine, cooked and drained

Preheat oven to 500°F (260°C). Use tomatoes held at room temperature until fully ripe. Core; cut into wedges. Place in a single layer on shallow baking pans; sprinkle with 2 tbs oil and all of the black pepper. Roast until edges are well browned, about 20 minutes; set aside.

In large skillet heat remaining 2 tbs oil until hot; add onions, garlic and oregano; sauté until tender, 4-5 minutes. Add wine; stir to loosen particles in pan; stir in parsley, red pepper and salt. Stir in reserved tomatoes and pan juices; cook until hot, about 2 minutes.

Opposite: Roasted Tomato Sauce with Fettucine and Herbs

Divide fettuccine among serving plates. Ladle 1 cup sauce over each portion. Serve with grated Parmesan cheese, if desired. Serves 24.

Approximate nutritional analysis per serving: Calories 430, Protein 12 g, Carbohydrates 61 g, Fat 17 g, Sodium 596 mg

Courtesy of the Florida Tomato Committee.

ZITI WITH MOZZARELLA AND PARMESAN CHEESE

1 lb (455 g) DE CECCO Ziti cut
2 cups (480 ml) diced mozzarella
⅓ cup (80 ml) butter
1 cup (240 ml) grated Parmesan cheese
salt
freshly ground black pepper

Cook the DE CECCO Ziti cut for 9 minutes in boiling salted water and drain. Season piping hot with the butter and Parmesan cheese diluted in a little pasta cooking water. Add the diced mozzarella, sprinkle generously with freshly ground black pepper and serve. You may like to add a little more grated Parmesan cheese at the table. Serves 6.

Approximate nutritional analysis per serving: Calories 658, Protein 31 g, Carbohydrates 59 g, Fat 33 g, Cholesterol 100 mg, Sodium 698 mg

TRI-COLOR PEPPER LINGUINE

1 medium green pepper, cut into thin strips
1 medium red pepper, cut into thin strips
1 medium yellow pepper, cut into thin strips
½ cup (120 ml) green onions, cut in 1-inch pieces
2 large cloves garlic, minced
2 tbs (30 ml) chopped fresh basil *or* 2 tsp (10 ml) dried basil leaves
2 tbs (30 ml) FLEISCHMANN'S Margarine
1 lb (455 g) linguine, cooked in unsalted water and drained
1 cup (240 ml) EGG BEATERS Real Egg Product
¼ cup (60 ml) grated Parmesan cheese

In skillet over medium-high heat, cook peppers, onions, garlic and basil in margarine until peppers are tender-crisp. In large serving bowl, toss peppers with hot linguine, egg product and cheese. Serve immediately. Serves 8.

Approximate nutritional analysis per serving: Calories 274, Fat 6 g, Cholesterol 56 mg, Sodium 125 mg

SAUCE NIÇOISE

1½ lbs (685 g) fresh FLORIDA
    tomatoes
2 tbs (30 ml) vegetable oil
¾ cup (180 ml) sliced onion
1 tsp (5 ml) crushed garlic
1 cup (240 ml) chicken broth
1¼ tsp (6 ml) thyme leaves,
    crushed
½ tsp (3 ml) salt
⅛ tsp (.5 ml) ground black
    pepper
1 - 9 oz pkg (270 g) frozen
    artichoke quarters, defrosted
½ cup (120 ml) sliced ripe olives
8 oz (240 g) fettuccine, cooked
    and drained

Use tomatoes held at room temperature until fully ripe. Core and cut tomatoes into 1-inch chunks; set aside. In a large skillet heat until hot. Add onion and garlic; cook until tender, about 4 minutes. Stir in chicken broth, thyme, salt, black pepper and reserved tomatoes; cook, uncovered, until tomatoes are slightly softened, about 4 minutes. Mix in artichokes; cook for 2 minutes. Stir in olives; heat until artichokes are tender and olives are hot, about 1 minute. Serve over hot cooked fettuccine. Serves 4.

Note: For a smoother sauce, tomatoes and artichokes can be coarsely chopped before cooking.

Approximate nutritional analysis per serving:
Calories 386, Protein 12 g,
Carbohydrates 56 g, Fat 14 g,
Cholesterol 53 mg, Sodium 697 mg

RONZONI LINGUINE À LA LEBOW

¾ cup (180 ml) half-and-half
¾ cup (180 ml) milk
1½ tsp (8 ml) grated lemon peel
1 tbs (15 ml) butter or margarine
3 cups (8 oz) (240 g) sliced and
    halved fresh mushrooms
2 tbs (30 ml) grated Parmesan
    cheese
8 oz (240 g) RONZONI Linguine,
    cooked
2 tbs (30 ml) chopped fresh
    parsley

In small saucepan, over medium heat, add half-and-half, milk and lemon peel; heat to boiling. Reduce heat to low; simmer until reduced in half, about 25 minutes. In large skillet, melt butter; add mushrooms. Cook until lightly browned. Add reduced half-and-half mixture and Parmesan cheese; mix well. Meanwhile, cook pasta according to package directions; drain. Toss hot pasta and sauce. Sprinkle with chopped parsley; serve immediately. Serves 4.

Approximate nutritional analysis per serving:
Calories 340 , Protein 12 g,
Carbohydrates 49 g, Fat 11 g,
Cholesterol 30 mg, Sodium 130 mg

Sauce Niçoise

FRESH TOMATO SAUCE WITH PINE NUTS AND RAISINS

2 ½ lbs (1.1 kg) fresh FLORIDA
    tomatoes
2 tbs (30 ml) vegetable oil
1 cup (5 oz) (150 g) onion,
    chopped
1 tsp (5 ml) garlic, crushed
1 ¼ tsp (6 ml) salt
1 tsp (5 ml) sugar
½ tsp (3 ml) ground allspice
⅔ cup (160 ml) golden raisins
⅔ cup (160 ml) pine nuts
    (pignolias), toasted*

Use tomatoes held at room temperature until fully ripe. Core tomatoes; chop; set aside. In a large skillet heat oil until hot. Add onion and garlic; cook and stir until crisp-tender, 3-4 minutes. Add reserved tomatoes, salt, sugar and allspice; simmer uncovered until sauce thickens, 10-12 minutes, stirring occasionally. Stir in raisins and pine nuts; cook until hot, about 1 minute. Serve over cooked fettuccine, if desired. Serves 4.

    * To toast pine nuts, place in a small skillet; cook over low heat, stirring frequently until golden brown, about 5 minutes.

Approximate nutritional analysis per serving:
Calories 332, Protein 9 g,
Carbohydrates 39 g, Fat 20 g,
Cholesterol 0 mg, Sodium 714 mg

Fresh Tomato Sauce with
Pine Nuts and Raisins

CREAMY PASTA PRIMAVERA

1 lb (455 g) fresh asparagus, cleaned, cut into 1-inch bits
2 cups (480 ml) fresh broccoli flowerettes
½ lb (230 g) fresh mushrooms, cleaned, cut in half
½ cup (120 ml) red or orange pepper strips
2 tbs (30 ml) chopped fresh chives
coarsely ground black pepper
1 cup (240 ml) nonfat sour cream alternative
½ cup (120 ml) shredded carrot
1 - 8 oz pkg (240 g) HEALTHY CHOICE Fat Free Natural Fancy Shredded Cheddar Cheese
12 oz (360 g) thin spaghetti, cooked, drained

Steam asparagus, broccoli, mushrooms and pepper until crisp-tender. Toss with chives; season to taste with pepper. Combine sour cream alternative, carrot, and half of cheese. Toss with cooked spaghetti; arrange on serving platter. Top with vegetable mixture; sprinkle with remaining cheese. Serves 8.

Approximate nutritional analysis per serving: Calories 239, Protein 10 g, Carbohydrates 38 g, Fat 1 g, Cholesterol 5 mg, Sodium 234 mg

Creamy Pasta Primavera

LINGUINE FLORENTINE

12 oz (360 g) thin linguine
4 tbs (60 ml) butter or margarine
3 shallots, minced
8 oz (240 g) fresh mushrooms,
**   sliced**
10 oz (300 g) fresh spinach,
**   coarsely chopped**
½ tsp (3 ml) McCORMICK or
**   SCHILLING**
**   Pure Anise Extract**
1 cup (240 ml) heavy cream
½ cup (120 ml) grated Parmesan
**   cheese**

Cook linguine, drain and return to pot.
While linguine is cooking, melt butter
in a large skillet over medium-high
heat. Add shallots and mushrooms;
sauté 2 minutes. Add spinach and sauté
2 minutes more. Add to drained
linguine and toss. Combine extract and
cream and toss with linguine along with
the Parmesan cheese. Toss until all
ingredients are warm and well blended.
Serves 4.

Approximate nutritional analysis per serving:
Calories 700, Protein 20 g,
Carbohydrates 69 g, Fat 39 g,
Cholesterol 122 mg, Sodium 435 mg

ALFREDO PASTA SAUCE

1 - 10 oz pkg (300 g) soft tofu,
**   drained**
1 medium clove garlic
3 tbs (45 ml) Parmesan cheese,
**   grated**
2 tbs (30 ml) Romano cheese,
**   grated**
2 tbs (30 ml) soy oil
¼ tsp (1 ml) white pepper
1 tsp (5 ml) onion powder
1 tsp (5 ml) basil
1 tbs (15 ml) dried parsley
12 oz (360 g) fettuccine, cooked
**   and drained**

In a blender or food processor, combine all ingredients except fettuccine.
Blend until creamy, about 30 seconds
on high. Heat sauce and serve over hot
cooked fettuccine. Serves 4.

Approximate nutritional analysis per 4 tbs
serving sauce: Calories 101, Protein 8 g,
Carbohydrates 3 g, Fat 6 g, Cholesterol 6 mg,
Sodium 133 mg

Courtesy of the United Soybean Board

Alfredo Pasta Sauce

SOUTHWESTERN PASTA SAUCE

2 medium onions, sliced
1 clove garlic, minced
¼ cup (60 ml) olive oil
1 - 28 oz can (840 g) tomatoes,
crushed or coarsely chopped
¾ tsp (4 ml) TABASCO sauce
¼ tsp (1 ml) salt
2-3 tbs (30-45 ml) fresh cilantro,
minced
¼ tsp (1 ml) granulated sugar
12 oz (360 g) angel hair pasta,
cooked and drained
grated Parmesan cheese,
optional

Heat oil over medium heat in a large, heavy non-aluminum saucepan. Stir in onions and garlic; sauté 10-12 minutes, stirring occasionally, until tender. Add tomatoes, TABASCO pepper sauce, salt, cilantro and sugar; bring to a boil. Reduce heat to low and simmer uncovered 30 minutes until slightly thickened. Place hot cooked pasta on heated serving platter; top with sauce. Sprinkle with Parmesan cheese if desired. Serves 4.

Approximate nutritional analysis per serving:
Calories 490, Protein 13 g,
Carbohydrates 74 g, Fat 16 g,
Cholesterol 0 mg, Sodium 470 mg

FETTUCCINE WITH MIXED GREENS

CREAMY MIXTURE:
12 oz (360 g) nonfat cottage
cheese
1 - 5 oz can (150 ml) evaporated
skim milk
3 tbs (45 ml) balsamic vinegar
3 tbs (45 ml) all-purpose flour

3 cups (720 ml) chopped onions
1 cup (240 ml) chopped celery
2 tbs (30 ml) CHEF PAUL
PRUDHOMME'S
Vegetable Magic, in all
1 cup (240 ml) apple juice
4 cups (960 ml) chopped fresh
mushrooms
4 cups (960 ml) chopped mustard
greens
4 cups (960 ml) chopped collard
greens
4 cups (960 ml) chopped chard
3½ cups (840 ml) vegetable stock
3 cups (720 ml) cooked fettuccine

Place the creamy mixture ingredients in a blender and puree until smooth and creamy; set aside.

Preheat a heavy 5-qt pot, preferably nonstick, over high heat to 350°F (180°C), about 4 minutes. Add the onions, celery, and 1 tbs of the Vegetable Magic and cook, checking the bottom of the pot occasionally for sticking, until the vegetables start to brown, about 8 minutes. Add the apple juice, clear the bottom of the pot of any brown bits, then add the mushrooms and remaining Vegetable Magic. Stir and cook until most of the liquid evaporates, about 7-8 minutes. Add all the greens and 3 cups of the stock, stir, and cook 6 minutes. Add the puréed creamy mixture and stir well.

CAUTION: Dishes using these creamy mixtures can "break" or curdle easily if they are brought to a full boil. Therefore, bring the liquid just to a gentle boil, stir immediately, then reduce the heat to low and simmer, stirring occasionally, for 10 minutes. Add the remaining ½ cup stock, stir, and add the fettuccine. Stir and cook until the pasta is heated throughout, about 5-6 minutes. Serve immediately. Serves 4.

Approximate nutritional analysis per serving:
Calories 392, Protein 23 g,
Carbohydrates 73 g, Fat 2 g, Sodium 726 mg

Opposite: Southwestern Pasta Sauce

PASTA E FAGIOLI

2 cans GOYA White Kidney
    Beans, drained
4 tbs (60 ml) GOYA Extra Virgin
    Olive Oil
1 large onion, chopped
1 clove garlic, minced
2 cups (480 ml) canned plum
    tomatoes
1 cup (240 ml) macaroni, cooked
fresh basil to taste
¼ tsp (1 ml) dry basil
½ tsp (3 ml) salt
black pepper, few grains
grated Parmesan cheese

Heat oil in 2-qt saucepan; add onion
and garlic and sauté until onion is
tender. Add tomatoes and simmer
10 minutes. Combine beans, cooked
macaroni, basil, salt and pepper. Bring
to a boil. Serve hot. Garnish with
Parmesan cheese. Serves 4.

*Approximate nutritional analysis per serving:
Calories 433, Protein 17 g,
Carbohydrates 60 g, Fat 15 g,
Cholesterol 0 mg, Sodium 1336 mg*

PASTA WITH ROASTED GARDEN VEGETABLES AND HERBS

1 each red, green and yellow bell
    pepper, quartered,
    seeds removed and cut into
    ½-inch wide strips
2 red onions, cut into ½-inch
    wide wedges
2 yellow squash, trimmed,
    in ½-inch slices
1 small eggplant trimmed,
    in 1-inch chunks
4 garlic cloves, peeled and halved
¼ cup (60 ml) BERTOLLI Extra
    Virgin Olive Oil
¼ cup (60 ml) finely chopped
    Italian parsley
2 tsp (10 ml) chopped fresh
    thyme leaves,
    stripped from stems
salt and freshly ground pepper
12 oz (360 g) penne, radiatore or
    other pasta
1 tbs (15 ml) grated Parmesan
    cheese

Preheat oven to 400°F (205°C). Spread
vegetables in a large roasting pan; add
olive oil; toss to coat. Bake, turning
often, until browned and tender, about
40 minutes. Add half of the parsley,
thyme, salt and pepper. Cook pasta in
large pot of boiling salted water until
cooked to taste. Ladle out ½ cup of the
pasta cooking liquid; reserve. Drain
pasta. In serving bowl toss pasta with
half the vegetables, cooking liquid and
cheese. Spoon remaining vegetables
and parsley on top. Serves 4.

*Approximate nutritional analysis per serving:
Calories 514, Protein 14 g,
Carbohydrates 80 g, Fat 16 g,
Cholesterol 1 mg, Sodium 46 mg*

QUICK HOMEMADE RED SAUCE

2 tbs (30 ml) GOYA Olive Oil
1 cup (240 ml) diced onions
1 cup (240 ml) diced carrots
1 tbs (15 ml) minced garlic
2 tbs (30 ml) GOYA Sofrito
4 - 8 oz cans (960 ml) GOYA
    Tomato Sauce
1 tsp (5 ml) oregano

In medium saucepan, heat oil and sauté
vegetables until golden. Add remaining
ingredients, cover, bring to boil and
simmer 15 minutes. Yields 4 cups.

*Approximate nutritional analysis per ½ cup
serving: Calories 64, Protein 1 g,
Carbohydrates 8 g, Fat 4 g,
Cholesterol 0 mg, Sodium 87 mg*

*Opposite: Pasta with Roasted
Garden Vegetables and Herbs*

BROCCOLI-TUNA PASTA TOSS

16 oz (450 g) spaghetti
1 - 10 oz pkg (300 g) frozen cut
    broccoli
1 - 10¾ oz can (325 ml)
    condensed cream of chicken
    soup
1 - 8 oz can (240 g) sliced water
    chestnuts, drained
½ cup (120 ml) DANNON Plain
    Nonfat or Lowfat Yogurt
½ cup (2 oz) (60 g) shredded
    cheddar cheese
1 tsp (5 ml) Worcestershire sauce
¼ tsp (1 ml) garlic powder
1 - 9¼ oz can (280 g) tuna packed
    in water, flaked

Cook pasta according to package
directions, adding frozen broccoli the
last 5-7 minutes of cooking; drain well.
Return pasta and broccoli to saucepan;
cover and keep warm.

In medium bowl combine soup,
water chestnuts, yogurt, cheese,
Worcestershire sauce and garlic
powder. Stir soup mixture into saucepan with drained pasta and broccoli.
Gently fold in tuna, being careful not to
break up large pieces. Cook over
medium-low heat about 5 minutes or
until heated through, stirring once or
twice. Serve immediately. Serves 5.

Approximate nutritional analysis per serving:
Calories 306, Protein 22 g,
Carbohydrates 35 g, Fat 9 g,
Cholesterol 25 mg, Sodium 815 mg.

Broccoli-Tuna Pasta Toss

LEMON-GARLIC ANGEL HAIR

3 large heads garlic
cooking spray
3 tbs (45 ml) GREY POUPON
    Dijon Mustard
2 tbs (30 ml) lemon juice
1/8 tsp (.5 ml) ground black
    pepper
2 cups (480 ml) cut-up fresh
    vegetables (snow peas,
    mushrooms, broccoli,
    carrots)
1 tbs (15 ml) FLEISCHMANN'S
    Margarine
1/2 cup (120 ml) water
8 oz (240 g) angel hair pasta,
    cooked and drained

Spray each head of garlic lightly with cooking spray; wrap each separately in foil. Place in small baking pan; bake at 400°F (205°C) for 45 minutes. Cool 10 minutes. Separate cloves; squeeze cloves to extract pulp (discard skins).

In food processor or electric blender, puree garlic pulp, mustard, lemon juice and pepper; set aside. In skillet, over medium-high heat, sauté vegetables in margarine until tender-crisp; add garlic mixture and water. Reduce heat to low; cook and stir until sauce is heated through. Toss with hot cooked angel hair. Serve immediately. Serves 4.

Approximate nutritional analysis per serving: Calories 387, Fat 6 g, Cholesterol 0 mg, Sodium 398 mg

CLASSIC SPAGHETTI SAUCE

2½ oz (75 g) dried mushrooms*
1½ cups (355 ml) water
1 lb (455 g) ground round or
    chuck
1 lb (455 g) Italian sausage
1 tbs (15 ml) sweet basil
1 tsp (5 ml) oregano
1 tbs (15 ml) marjoram
1-2 tbs (15-30 ml) salt
1 tsp (5 ml) fresh ground black
    pepper
3 chopped onions
3 chopped green peppers
2 - 6 oz cans (360 g) LIBBY'S
    Tomato Paste
2 - 28 oz cans (1.7 kg) LIBBY'S
    Whole Peeled
    Tomatoes in juice
1½ cups (355 ml) dry red wine
3 bay leaves
2 tbs (30 ml) olive oil
7 cloves garlic, sliced
1 cup (240 ml) fresh chopped
    parsley

* ½ lb (230 g) fresh mushrooms or
1 - 6 oz can (180 g) can be substituted
but flavor will be altered.

Soak mushrooms in 1½ cups water at least 15 minutes. In large skillet, brown ground round and sausage adding basil, oregano, marjoram, 1 tbs salt and pepper. Transfer to a large soup or sauce pan; mix in onions and green peppers.

Add tomato paste; heat and mix thoroughly. Add tomatoes, mushrooms with liquid, 1 cup red wine and bay leaves. Simmer for 1 hour, taste and add up to 1 tbs more of salt if needed. Cook for another 1½ hours. In a small frying pan, heat olive oil and brown garlic. Add this to sauce along with ½ cup red wine and parsley. Continue cooking for another 30 minutes before removing from heat. Taste for additional seasoning. Yields 3½ qts.

Approximate nutritional analysis per 1 cup serving: Calories 338, Protein 18 g, Carbohydrates 15 g, Fat 21 g, Cholesterol 62 mg, Sodium 1275 mg

Classic Spaghetti Sauce

ROBUST RED BEANS AND BOWTIES

2 tbs (30 ml) GOYA Olive Oil
1 lb (455 g) Italian sausage
1 cup (240 ml) LA VINA Red Cooking Wine
1 - 10 oz pkg (300 g) frozen chopped broccoli, thawed and drained
1 recipe QUICK HOMEMADE RED SAUCE (page 10) *or* 1 - 26 oz jar (780 ml) prepared sauce
1 - 16 oz can (480 g) GOYA Red Kidney Beans
1 lb (455 g) bowties, cooked and drained

In large hot skillet, heat 1 tsp oil. Brown sausages on all sides, breaking apart. Add wine, lower flame, cover and simmer until wine is absorbed. Set aside on plate to cool. Sauté broccoli in 1 tbs oil. Add sausage, sauce and beans. Cover and boil. Lower flame and simmer 10 minutes. Stir in bowties and heat thoroughly. Serves 8.

Approximate nutritional analysis per serving: Calories 598, Protein 25 g, Carbohydrates 63 g, Fat 26 g, Cholesterol 47 mg, Sodium 835 mg

QUICK AND SPICY PASTA DEL MAR

1 medium onion, diced
1 tsp (5 ml) olive oil
1 - 10 oz can (300 g) baby clams, drained
2 tsp (10 ml) minced garlic
1 - 26 oz jar (780 ml) HEALTHY CHOICE Traditional Pasta Sauce
1 tsp (5 ml) dried basil
½ tsp (3 ml) dried thyme
⅛ tsp (.5 ml) black pepper
⅛ tsp (.5 ml) cayenne pepper
½ lb (230 g) raw medium shrimp, peeled
½ lb (230 g) linguine, cooked and drained

In large saucepan, sauté onion in hot oil until tender. Add clams and garlic; cook and stir 1 minute longer. Stir in pasta sauce, basil, thyme, black pepper and cayenne pepper. Heat, stirring occasionally, until mixture comes to a boil. Add shrimp; reduce heat to medium; cook until shrimp are pink and cooked through. Serve sauce over linguine. Serves 6.

Approximate nutritional analysis per serving: Calories 278, Protein 28 g, Fat 3 g, Cholesterol 105 mg, Sodium 520 mg

PASTA CARBONARA

½ cup (120 ml) sliced CALIFORNIA ripe olives
½ cup (120 ml) sliced mushrooms
½ cup (120 ml) crumbled bacon
¼ cup (60 ml) minced scallion greens
½ tsp (3 ml) black pepper, coarse
3 tbs (45 ml) margarine
¾ cup (180 ml) grated Parmesan cheese
3 large eggs, beaten
1 cup (240 ml) whipping cream
7 oz (210 g) packaged linguine, cooked and drained

Combine first 5 ingredients in small bowl. Put margarine in 2-qt casserole. Microwave on HIGH for 1 minute. Add olive mixture. Microwave on HIGH for 1 minute. Add remaining ingredients. Mix well. Microwave on HIGH for 3-5 minutes, stirring once per minute, or until sauce is thickened. Serves 6.

Approximate nutritional analysis per serving: Calories 453, Protein 15 g, Carbohydrates 31 g, Fat 31 g, Cholesterol 174 mg, Sodium 591 mg

SEAFOOD FIESTA FETTUCINE

12 oz (360 g) fettucine
1½ cups (355 ml) part skim ricotta cheese
4 oz (120 g) feta cheese, crumbled
½ cup (120 ml) milk
6 scallions, thinly sliced
1 - 8¾ oz can (260 g) whole yellow corn, drained
2 medium tomatoes, seeded and diced
1 tsp (5 ml) McCORMICK or SCHILLING Garlic Powder
1 tbs (15 ml) McCORMICK or SCHILLING Basil Leaves
1 tsp (5 ml) McCORMICK or SCHILLING Butter Flavor
1 lb (455 g) combination cooked and peeled shrimp, scallops and crab meat

Cook pasta, drain and return to pot. While pasta is cooking, puree ricotta and feta cheese and milk in blender or food processor. Add to cooked pasta along with remaining ingredients, except seafood, and toss until all ingredients are warm. Serve on a platter topped with seafood. Serves 4.

Approximate nutritional analysis per serving: Calories 642, Protein 48 g, Carbohydrates 85 g, Fat 12 g, Cholesterol 205 mg, Sodium 448 mg

Pasta Carbonara

SHRIMP AND SCALLOP PASTA IN CHIVE-GINGER SAUCE

1 cup (240 ml) **BLUE DIAMOND
    Blanched Slivered Almonds**
3 tbs (45 ml) butter, divided
½ lb (230 g) medium, raw
    shrimp, shelled and deveined
½ lb (230 g) scallops (if large,
    slice into medallions)
2 cloves garlic, chopped finely
1 tsp (5 ml) grated, fresh ginger
    or ⅛ tsp (.5 ml) powdered
    ginger
3 cups (720 ml) heavy cream
¼ cup (60 ml) thinly sliced, fresh
    chives
    or 1 tbs (15 ml) dried chives
1 tbs (15 ml) lemon juice
1 tsp (5 ml) grated lemon peel
½ tsp (3 ml) salt
¼ tsp (1 ml) white pepper
1 lb (455 g) fresh fettucine,
    cooked and drained
    or 8 oz (240 g) dried fettucine,
    cooked and drained

Sauté almonds in 1 tbs butter until golden; reserve. Slice shrimp in half lengthwise. Sauté scallops and shrimp in remaining 2 tbs butter over medium-high heat, about 2 minutes or until barely tender. Reserve. Mix garlic and ginger and cream. Cook over medium-high heat until sauce thickens and lightly coats the back of a spoon. Stir in chives, lemon juice, lemon peel, salt and pepper. Add seafood and heat through. Add almonds. Toss with hot, cooked pasta. Serves 4.

Approximate nutritional analysis per serving:
Calories 1205, Protein 39 g,
Carbohydrates 56 g, Fat 94 g,
Cholesterol 373 mg, Sodium 605 mg

*Shrimp and Scallop Pasta
in Chive-Ginger Sauce*

SILVERADO SEAFOOD PASTA

1 - 10 oz jar (300 g) fresh oysters, halved if large
½ lb (230 g) fresh scallops, cut up if large
½ lb (230 g) prawns, shelled and deveined
2 tbs (30 ml) bottled or fresh minced garlic
¼ cup (60 ml) butter or margarine
¼ cup (60 ml) olive oil
⅛-¼ tsp (.5-1 ml) ground saffron or saffron threads
¼ cup (60 ml) chopped fresh fennel or dill leaves
1 lb (455 g) Roma or regular tomatoes, chopped
1 cup (240 ml) CALIFORNIA ripe olive wedges
¼ cup (60 ml) dry white wine mixed with
1 tbs (15 ml) flour
8 oz (240 g) angel hair pasta (capellini)
3 tbs olive oil, to coat

Gently sauté oysters, scallops, prawns and garlic in butter and olive oil for 5 minutes or just until cooked. Add saffron, fennel, tomatoes and olives and cook a few minutes to heat; add wine-flour mixture and cook, stirring until thickened and glossy. Meanwhile, drop pasta into a large pot of boiling water and boil for 3 minutes; drain and toss with olive oil to coat. To serve, divide hot pasta into wide soup bowls, ladle seafood sauce over. Serves 4.

Approximate nutritional analysis per serving: Calories 657, Protein 35 g, Carbohydrates 55 g, Fat 32 g, Cholesterol 178 mg, Sodium 576 mg

PENNE ALLA NAPOLITANA

12 oz (360 g) penne or other small tubular pasta
4 tbs (60 ml) virgin olive oil, divided
2 tbs (30 ml) finely chopped garlic
1 cup (240 ml) pitted CALIFORNIA ripe olives, sliced
¼ cup (60 ml) packed fresh basil leaves, coarsely chopped
1 tsp (5 ml) bottled red pepper flakes
2 cups (480 ml) Homemade Fresh Tomato Sauce
½ cup (120 ml) mozzarella cheese, ¼-inch cubed
½ cup (120 ml) grated Parmesan cheese

HOMEMADE FRESH TOMATO SAUCE:
2 tbs (30 ml) olive oil
¾ cup (180 ml) chopped onion
3 lbs (1.4 kg) tomatoes, seeded and chopped
1 tbs (15 ml) minced garlic
9 fresh basil sprigs
salt and pepper

Pasta: Drop penne into pan of boiling water, return to boil and boil gently for 8-10 minutes or until al dente (tender but still with a firm bite). Drain, toss with 1 tbs olive oil, return to pan and keep warm.

SAUCE: Sauté garlic slowly in 3 tbs olive oil in skillet until softened but not browned. Add olives, basil, red pepper and tomato sauce. Heat. Stir in cheeses and heat, stirring, until chunks begin to melt. Pour over pasta. Pass additional grated Parmesan cheese to sprinkle over if desired. Serves 4.

HOMEMADE FRESH TOMATO SAUCE: Heat olive oil in skillet, add onions and sauté until translucent. Add tomatoes, garlic and whole basil sprigs. Cook, covered over medium heat for 45 minutes to 1 hour or until saucy.
Add salt and pepper to taste.
Yields 3⅔ cups.

Approximate nutritional analysis per serving: Calories 661, Protein 23 g, Carbohydrates 78 g, Fat 29 g, Cholesterol 30 mg, Sodium 147 mg

SHRIMP AND PASTA POMPEIAN

¼ cup (60 ml) POMPEIAN Extra
    Virgin Olive Oil
1 clove garlic, minced
1 tbs (15 ml) dried basil
1 tbs (15 ml) dried oregano
1 green sweet bell pepper,
    chopped
1 tsp (5 ml) dried parsley flakes
⅛ tsp (.5 ml) fennel seeds,
    optional
1 lb (455 g) raw shrimp, peeled
    and deveined
1 - 8 oz can (240 g) tomato paste
1 medium onion, chopped
1 tsp (5 ml) sugar
¼ tsp (1 ml) freshly ground
    pepper
⅛ tsp (.5 ml) cayenne
1 - 14½ oz can (435 g) Italian
    plum tomatoes, chopped
1 lb (455 g) cooked linguine
    tossed with
2 tbs (30 ml) POMPEIAN Extra
    Virgin Olive Oil

Place the extra virgin olive oil, garlic,
onion and bell pepper in a medium
saucepan, cook 5 minutes, stirring
occasionally. Add remaining ingredients except for the shrimp and linguine.
Simmer uncovered for 15 minutes.
Add the prepared shrimp, cover and
simmer 5 minutes. Serve over hot
cooked linguine. Serves 4.

Approximate nutritional analysis per serving:
Calories 825, Protein 42 g,
Carbohydrates 110 g, Fat 25 g,
Cholesterol 172 mg, Sodium 416 mg

MEDITERRANEAN SEAFOOD PASTA WITH SMOKED TOMATO PESTO

2 tbs (30 ml) olive oil
1 clove garlic, minced
1 medium red or green bell
    pepper, cut into thin strips
¼ cup (60 ml) dry white wine
8 oz (240 g) seafood (shrimp,
    scallops, crabmeat
    or lobster)
¼ cup (60 ml) sliced ripe olives
1 - 9 oz pkg (270 g) CONTADINA
    Refrigerated Linguine,
    cooked, drained and
    kept warm
1 - 7 oz container (210 g)
    CONTADINA Refrigerated
    Pesto with Sun Dried
    Tomatoes, slightly warmed
1 tbs (15 ml) capers
1 oz (30 g) crumbled feta cheese

In medium skillet, heat oil; sauté garlic
1-2 minutes. Add bell pepper; sauté for
2 minutes. Add wine and shrimp; sauté
2-3 minutes. Stir in olives. In medium
bowl, toss pasta with pesto. To serve,
divide onto plates; top with shrimp and
vegetable mixture. Sprinkle with capers
and feta cheese. Serves 4.

Approximate nutritional analysis per serving:
Calories 526, Protein 22 g,
Carbohydrates 42 g, Fat 30 g,
Cholesterol 95 mg, Sodium 349 mg

Opposite: Shrimp and
Pasta Pompeian

Mediterranean Seafood Pasta
with Smoked Tomato Pesto

CAMP CABIN "LASAGNE"

6 oz (180 g) elbow or cartwheel
    macaroni
1 - 8 oz can (240 ml) tomato sauce
1 - 6 oz pkg (180 g) sliced jack or
    cheddar cheese
1 small tomato, cubed
½ pt container (240 ml) lowfat
    ricotta cheese
1½ tsp (8 ml) thyme
½ cup (120 ml) CALIFORNIA ripe
    olive slices
½ cup (120 ml) sour cream

Drop macaroni into boiling water in
pot about 8 inches in diameter and
2½-qt capacity. Cover, return to boil
and simmer 7 minutes or until done.
Drain and remove from pot. Pour
tomato sauce into bottom of pot. Make
layer of macaroni on sauce, then layer
sliced cheese, tomato, ricotta, thyme,
olives and sour cream, in that order.
Cover and place over low heat for 20
minutes or until bubbling at edges and
hot in center. Serves 4.

Approximate nutritional analysis per serving:
Calories 604, Protein 32 g,
Carbohydrates 47 g, Fat 32 g,
Cholesterol 95 mg, Sodium 577 mg

Camp Cabin "Lasagne"

CREAMY CHICKEN PRIMAVERA

2 cups (480 ml) water
1 cup (240 ml) diced carrots
1 cup (240 ml) broccoli flowerets
1 cup (240 ml) tri-color rotini
    pasta
½ lb (230 g) cooked chicken, cut
    into cubes
½ cup (120 ml) DANNON Plain
    Nonfat or Lowfat Yogurt
¼ cup (60 ml) finely chopped
    green onions, green part only
2 tbs plus 2 tsp (40 ml) reduced-
    calorie mayonnaise
½ tsp (3 ml) dried basil, crushed
⅛ tsp (.5 ml) pepper
carrot curls, optional

In a medium saucepan combine water, carrots and broccoli. Cook, covered, 10-15 minutes or until tender-crisp; drain. Cook pasta according to package directions; rinse and drain. In a large bowl combine pasta, carrots and broccoli. Toss gently.

    In a small bowl combine chicken, yogurt, green onions, mayonnaise, basil and pepper; mix well. Add to pasta mixture. Toss gently to combine. Cover; chill several hours. If desired, garnish with carrot curls. Serves 4.

Approximate nutritional analysis per serving:
Calories 468, Protein 35 g,
Carbohydrates 72 g, Fat 9 g,
Cholesterol 60 mg, Sodium 256 mg

LASAGNE WITH WHITE SAUCE

¾ cup (180 ml) 1% lowfat cottage
    cheese
¾ cup (180 ml) part-skim ricotta
    cheese
¼ cup (60 ml) EGG BEATERS
    Real Egg Product
1 tsp (5 ml) Italian seasoning
⅓ cup (80 ml) chopped onion
1 clove garlic, minced
1 tbs (15 ml) FLEISCHMANN'S
    Margarine
1 tbs (15 ml) all purpose flour
⅔ cup (160 ml) skim milk
1½ cups (355 ml) thinly sliced
    zucchini
½ cup (120 ml) shredded carrots
¼ cup (60 ml) shredded
    Parmesan cheese
6 lasagna noodles, cooked and
    drained
¾ cup (180 ml) shredded
    part-skim mozzarella cheese

In medium bowl, combine cottage cheese, ricotta cheese, egg product and Italian seasoning; set aside.

    In large skillet, over medium heat, sauté onion and garlic in margarine until tender; stir in flour. Add milk, stirring until thickened; cook and stir 1 minute more. Stir in zucchini, carrots and 2 tbs Parmesan cheese; set aside.

    Spray 10x6x2-inch baking dish with nonstick cooking spray. Arrange 2 noodles in dish; spread with ⅓ cottage cheese mixture, ⅓ zucchini mixture and sprinkle with ⅓ mozzarella cheese. Repeat layers, starting with noodles, 2 more times; sprinkle with remaining 2 tbs Parmesan cheese. Bake, uncovered, at 350°F (180°C) for 35 minutes or until heated through. Let stand 10 minutes before serving. Serves 6.

Approximate nutritional analysis per serving:
Calories 257, Protein 20 g,
Carbohydrates 42 g, Fat 8 g,
Cholesterol 22 mg, Sodium 334 mg

Lasagne with
White Sauce

MOM'S LEAN AND QUICK LASAGNE

1 cup (240 ml) chopped onion
1 tbs (15 ml) vegetable oil
½ lb (230 g) extra lean
    ground beef or
    ground turkey breast
1 - 26 oz jar (780 ml) HEALTHY
    CHOICE Traditional
    Pasta Sauce
1 - 15 oz carton (450 g) part-skim
    ricotta cheese
¼ cup (60 ml) grated Parmesan
    cheese
½ tsp (3 ml) dried basil
½ tsp (3 ml) dried oregano
6 lasagna noodles, cooked,
    drained
1 ½ cups (355 ml) HEALTHY
    CHOICE Fat Free
    Mozzarella Shreds

In large nonstick saucepan, sauté onion in hot oil until tender. Add ground beef, and brown until cooked through. Stir in pasta sauce; heat through. In small bowl, mix together ricotta and Parmesan cheeses with basil and oregano. In 13x9x2-inch baking dish, layer 3 noodles, half of cheese mixture, half of sauce and half of mozzarella cheese. Repeat layers. Bake at 350°F (180°C) for 30 minutes. Serves 8.

Approximate nutritional analysis per serving: Calories 270, Fat 9 g, Cholesterol 38 mg, Sodium 561 mg

SPINACH, SAUSAGE AND OLIVE ROLL

½ lb (230 g) hot or mild Italian
    sausage
olive oil
1 ½ tsp (8 ml) fennel seed
¾ cup (180 ml) chopped onion
⅓ cup (80 ml) chopped fresh
    basil
¾ cup (180 ml) coarsely chopped
    CALIFORNIA ripe olives
1 - 10 oz pkg frozen chopped
    spinach, thawed
1 cup (240 ml) ricotta cheese
2 eggs
salt and pepper to taste
2 sheets fresh egg pasta, about
    12x10 inches each
1 cup (240 ml) grated mozzarella
    cheese
basil sprigs, optional
fresh tomato sauce

Remove sausage from casings and crumble into oiled skillet. Sprinkle with fennel seed and cook until brown. Remove from pan and drain off most of fat. Add onions and sauté until tender. Add basil and sauté 1-2 minutes longer. Combine onions and basil, sausage and olives; cool. Squeeze spinach as dry as possible. Mix well with ricotta and eggs then add to sausage mixture. Add salt and pepper to taste.

Gently unroll pasta and, if coated with flour, brush off excess. Place one sheet of pasta in large colander in sink. Gently pour boiling water over to moisten and soften. Gently rinse with cold water then carefully slip from colander onto large sheet of oiled foil on counter. Repeat with other sheet of pasta.

Spread each sheet of pasta with half the ricotta mixture, leaving a 1-inch border at long edges. Sprinkle with mozzarella and roll up, starting from long edge. Wrap foil around and twist ends to enclose. Place wrapped rolls in wide baking pan and bake at 350°F (180°C) for 25 minutes or until center reads at least 145°F (63°C) on instant (probe-style) thermometer.* Cool rolls 10 minutes in wrap then unwrap and slice. Pour fresh tomato sauce onto plates, add pasta spirals and garnish with basil sprigs. Serves 6.

    * If you don't have a thermometer, unwrap roll and make a small cut in center to see if it is hot enough.

Approximate nutritional analysis per serving: Calories 777, Protein 36 g, Carbohydrates 103 g, Fat 24 g, Cholesterol 128 mg, Sodium 1528 mg

***Opposite: Spinach, Sausage
and Olive Roll***

CHEF PAUL'S MACARONI AND CHEESE

1½ cups (355 ml) **chopped onions**
¾ cup (180 ml) **chopped celery**
2 tbs plus 1 tsp (35 ml) **CHEF PAUL PRUDHOMME'S Pork and Veal Magic**
½ cup (120 ml) **defatted chicken stock, in all**
5 **egg whites**
1 - 12 oz container (360 g) **low-fat cottage cheese**
1 - 12 oz can (360 ml) **evaporated skim milk**
1-2 tsp (5-10 ml) **salt, optional**
10 cups (2.4 L) **cooked small elbow macaroni**
6 oz (180 g) **low-fat cheddar cheese (7 g fat per oz), shredded**

Preheat oven to 375°F (190°C).

Heat a 10-inch skillet over high heat. Add chopped onions, celery and Pork and Veal Magic. Cook 2 minutes, then stir to blend in seasoning. When vegetables begin to stick hard to the pan, about 2-3 minutes, add ¼ cup stock, scrape up the brown on the pan bottom, stir well and cook 1-2 minutes. Turn heat down to medium and stir. Cook until vegetables begin to stick hard again, about 4-5 minutes, and add the remaining ¼ cup stock. Scrape up pan bottom, stir well and continue cooking another 4-5 minutes. Remove from heat and let cool slightly.

Place the egg whites in food processor. Process 30-45 seconds, or until the egg whites are nice and frothy, but not until they make peaks. Add the cottage cheese and the milk and process. Don't let the mixture get too smooth; a bit of lumpiness in the cottage cheese will give the dish more texture. Add the cooled mixture from the skillet and process again, about 20 seconds. Taste and add salt if you desire. Place the cooked, drained macaroni into a bowl, pour the sauce over and mix well. Pour into an unbuttered casserole, sprinkle the cheddar cheese on top and bake for 35-40 minutes, or until brown and bubbly. Serves 10.

Approximate nutritional analysis per serving: Calories 303, Protein 20 g, Carbohydrates 47 g, Fat 4 g, Cholesterol 12 mg, Sodium 596 mg

Chef Paul's Macaroni and Cheese